TRANSCEND

Transcend
Living an Inspired Life

ERIKA DEGRAFFINREAIDT

ISBN 979-8-9950844-0-2 (hardback)
ISBN 979-8-9950844-2-6 (paperback)
ISBN 979-8-9950844-1-9 (ebook)

First paperback edition

CONTENTS

I present this book as a gift to my mother, twin brother, and older brother, whose love and support have allowed me to get through every season of my life thus far.

To my Granny, the matriarch, who, due to her strength, left the desolate South to give her family a better life, which, in turn, gave me a better life, showing that one decision made in a season can cause a ripple effect for generations.

To my nephews, extended family, and friends: this gift is for you!

Acknowledgements

Thank you, my Creator, my God, my Lord Jesus Christ, for enriching my life with the many experiences and gifts I have used to write this book and to be a testimony of Your goodness.

Thank you to my publisher and the editors who made this book possible with their knowledge and expertise. I am forever indebted to you.

To those who have been following my journey over these many years and have poured words of encouragement into me and offered prayers that have kept me pushing toward a greater purpose that led to *Transcend*: thank you!

Transcend. Open your eyes. Each day, you are given the opportunity to see anew, to breathe life through your lungs, and to speak affirmations over your existence. Not everyone gets this chance. I hope that, through this book, on your loneliest days, you find comfort; in the storm, you find peace; and in your darkness, you find hope.

- Erika Degraffinreaidt

Transcendence

I have had several seasons where I felt I had lived multiple lifetimes within each one. I have this one life throughout which I have experienced wins, losses, laughs, tears, blessings, and lessons that have transformed me into who I am in this moment. Through these internal and external changes, I can confidently say that I have *transcended*—a word that means to rise above something or a particular circumstance or way of being, primarily one deemed difficult or depleting. *Transcendence* also denotes the experience of art, whether through painting, music, writing, or a spiritual search.

Within these seasons, I not only experienced emotional and physical depletion from the challenges life threw at me, but I also fought those silent battles while continuing to encourage others. Recently, a colleague I had worked with eight years ago reached out to me through social media and shared that they had never had the opportunity to tell me that a compliment I had given to them had stuck with them to this day, and that, for the first time in their life, they had felt seen and understood during a time they had been struggling with simply being themselves. (For context, we worked in an environment where your looks determine whether you are the season's "It" person.) Hearing how I had made them feel many years ago was fulfilling, because in all honesty, the words I had spoken were ones I was yearning to hear regarding myself. That particular season of my life had been hard mentally, physically, financially, and emotionally. Being in my 20s and not yet feeling comfortable with who I was and wanting to be seen was overwhelming. This situation showed me that smiles can often hide the deepest sorrows, but positive words can serve as a bridge to transcendence. Throughout time, I have met many people and versions of myself that have caused me to think, tear through inner layers, and ask, *"Who am I, and who do I need to be?"* Transcending is about becoming free.

Throughout this book, I share personal stories to not only show our similarities as humans but also to help you through your journey of transcending. This book provides practical, everyday aspirations I created during my period of darkness that fed my soul and illuminated my inner light, which allowed me to break through the confines of my mind. As you read, I invite you to question who you *are* and who you *need* to be and start the process of transcending.

With each day we are given, there is constant change. As human beings, we are not meant to stay the same, but like a passing season, we evolve, improve, and grow, which in turn helps others to do the same.

Recently, someone told me that they felt they had seen three versions of me throughout the 10+ years of us knowing each other. They proceeded to tell me their perception of me when we first met in my early 20s. They described how I wore all black and the same "mohawk" hairstyle for *years* and always wore sunglasses indoors as well as outdoors at night. They also mentioned that I never smiled. How eye-opening it is to hear how someone perceives you, that what someone saw externally was how I felt internally. As I mentioned before, my early 20s were dark and uncomfortable. This person met me in my season of brokenness—it was evident—but in the darkness, God gave me hope, allowing me to keep moving forward while hiding me in plain sight.

The person proceeded to talk about the second version they had met. For context, we first met when I lived in Chicago. When we saw each other again, I was in my late 20s and living in New York. (This shows how God will take you through seasons and MOVE you in order to MOLD you and to GROW you into who you are truly meant to be.) They said that the second version of me was showing subtle signs of the first version, where I still wore sunglasses, but I had a new hairstyle and a new demeanor. I walked differently, I spoke eloquently; I was changing. Lastly, they said that the version of me that was standing in front of them (now in Los Angeles), they didn't recognize: "I feel," they said, "I need to be introduced to this new version of you." I laughed, extended my hand, and introduced myself with confidence, a smile, a new hairstyle, no sunglasses, no longer in hiding, and finally free—transcendent: *Hi, my name is Erika Degraffinreaidt.*

If you are ready for a life of transformation, then hold on tight and trust.

Part I

There is beauty in the Wait...

CHAPTER 1

The Waiting Room

Along this journey, over the course of many years, I have found myself in seasons of solitude, silence, and loneliness; seasons where, if I were in a room full of people and cried out, I felt I would only hear the echo of my voice. I remember thinking my loneliness was a punishment from God, that I must have done something wrong to have had not a soul to talk to. There were seasons when I would walk down the street and no one would smile at me. Some days, I wished someone would bring up the weather or ask about my day, but that never happened.

After spending time in the season that I now call *The Waiting Room,* I found myself—the self once hidden in darkness. I learned God was not punishing me; He was *molding* me, shaping me for a bigger purpose. He hid me so that when I emerged from the waiting room, out of my cocoon, I would, like a butterfly, showcase the inner beauty others once could not see.

Allow yourself to sit in the waiting room. Feel what you have long tried to avoid. Recognize the distractions you used to fill the voids you tried to escape. It is similar to the concept of an *escape room*, except the room is your life, and with each day, you are given a mission to achieve a specific goal. Sometimes the goal will seem unreachable, especially when facing challenges that seemingly look and feel good but lead to a dead end, a void.

There are many things we use to fill these voids; they show up in different forms. I call these forms the "Case of the HOL." *HOL* is a Dutch word for "hollow" or "cave," representing a hole or a cavity. Each form digs you into a hole (darkness) and makes you feel hollow (insignificant) or like a cavity (empty). I have experienced all of the HOLs listed below in one form or another, so I can say the following without judgment: without the HOLs, I would not have been brought to Light. (I have highlighted the most common HOLs as they are more easily recognizable, but the list goes on.)

AlcoHOLic

Alcohol affects our actions and our ability to make decisions; it distorts our reality.

WorkaHOLic

Working hard and long hours, compulsively, indicates a need to avoid our reality.

SexaHOLic

Sex addiction and needing excessive amounts of physical affection come from not feeling our own self-love.

ShopaHOLic

Compulsive shopping, or overbuying, in order to dress up the external, comes from trying to make ourselves feel good internally.

I have gone down those HOLs and built walls in hopes that I would be protected from whatever hurt I was going through in those seasons. As I kept feeding them, they led me further and further into darkness. I vividly remember nights when I kept feeding my body these things, and though they fulfilled me for a few hours, when I came out of the hole *(HOL)* I had dug, I felt even more empty and hurt. It took my crying out in the confines of my small, dimly lit apartment one night, against a picturesque Chicago skyline, for me to realize that to get rid of the HOL, I must starve it. I had an encounter with God that night that started a 13-year process of becoming unrecognizable to those who would encounter the future me—13 years of sitting in a waiting room.

If you have ever been in a waiting room, especially at a hospital, you know how uncomfortable it can be. Whether you are in physical pain, or anxious from wondering when your name will be called, or managing the discomfort of the hard, plastic chair, you sit and bear until it is your turn. Once your name is called, you look back and think *it wasn't that bad*, and most importantly, you see how you got through it. It also shows that there is beauty in the wait if you are willing to hold on. For me, I reached a point of desperation—wanting to feel *whole*, not *in a hole*. But transformation is a process; it can take months or years (13 in my case), but it is meant to bring us to the version of ourselves that we were called to be. If you know the symbolism of the number 13, you know why I continue to reiterate the number of years I waited in that room. Biblically, the number 13 is defined as a cycle of endings and a rebirth. This was my rebirth.

The escape room that came with its challenges was suddenly met with ease, not because the challenges became easier, but because it took the renewal of my mind and my surroundings and recognizing the people who kept feeding the beast within, deepening the HOLs. To *escape the room*, you must recognize the distractions, feel the pain, and heal. Sit in the waiting room, no matter how uncomfortable it may be, because once you come out, you will see that the wait was not a punishment: it was a preparation for who your future self is waiting on.

Reflect on a moment where you felt God had you in a waiting room. What things did you have to give up to become who you are today?

A Mind of Their Own...

CHAPTER 2

A Beautiful Mind

"The mind is a terrible thing to waste" is a saying that was once used as a form of reprimand from parents telling us that our actions were unacceptable, by instructors and professors as a way of saying *if you don't apply yourself, it's a squander,* and as a way of saying that our minds, when used for good, can take us places and bring us into spaces that can make the world rumble. But how does one know when to trust one's thoughts, or if one's thoughts are powerful enough to make the world take notice?

I have always been a thinker. I have always had a creative mind and style—a way of doing and saying things that, many times, only I could understand. Starting at a young age, many people thought my mind may have been under-developed, as I wasn't catching on to things as quickly as my peers. I didn't learn to read until I was in 2nd grade. I was able to pass kindergarten and 1st grade only by God's grace.

I was separated from my twin brother and my peers and placed in rooms by myself or with other "creative thinkers" because I was misunderstood. I still remember the day the principal sent a letter to my mother stating that, in my instructors'"professional opinion,"it was believed that I should be placed in a classroom with students who were intellectually disabled because my thoughts weren't in alignment with my peers'. I will never forget my mom crumpling up that paper and telling me, "There is nothing wrong with you." The instructors brought my mother and me into a classroom to further explain the issue, in hopes of convincing her that the new placement would be the "best" thing for me, but she stood her ground. My mother informed the instructors, in the most respectful way, that "there is nothing wrong with my child!"

So, I stayed with my peers. Though I may not have been the greatest academically, my mother knew, and those around me knew, that I put in effort. My heart and undying ability to not give up made others not want to give up on me. It was my mother's belief in me that allowed me to believe in myself and embrace how I was different and not feel afraid to share my thoughts. Her one decision in that season of my life caused a domino effect, placing me where I am right now. My mother knew my mind was not a waste and was not going to allow it to be thrown away by someone who could not understand my thought processes; she instilled my hope and belief in transcending.

The world will try to make you believe you are "delusional" for having a dream or not thinking in alignment with the thoughts of the masses. The dreams we have been given are not for us to harbor; they were placed in our beautiful minds to be realized—brought to fruition—to change not just our reality, but the realities of others. A beautiful mind is about persevering through life's many obstacles, which in some cases may come with suffering. Long-suffering is a gift from God; it has a higher purpose and an end.

You were created and placed on this earth to look, to speak, and to THINK differently. If you do not embrace this, how can you allow someone to see you? My mother saw me, and thanks to that, throughout my life, other people have been able to see my beautiful mind as a stylist, a designer, an actress, a photographer, and now a writer. It has stretched me into new realities and brought me into rooms with those whose thoughts align with my own—thoughts that are unlimited and minds that are open to seeing a world outside of their own. A beautiful mind, when fully explored, comes with resilience, hope, and the power of love. Give yourself permission to not just explore but to also fully embrace those elements, which, in turn, bring meaning to your purpose.

A purpose that was specifically and intentionally created by God for you, giving a reason for being, driving actions and giving life meaning. Could you imagine a world without the brilliant mind of Steve Jobs? His purpose was created, specifically for him, other individuals before him were not able to bring these innovations into fruition because it was not their purpose and the timing would have been off. As Ecclesiastes 3 (NIV) states, "There is a time for everything, and a season for every activity under the heavens." Steve's mind and thinking processes have been extensively studied and analyzed by psychologists, neuroscientists, biographers and business writers. All having their own hypothesis and theoretic formulas on how his mind came to be. When truly the only clear explanation is that it was the plan of God.

Steve's purpose has transformed industries throughout the world, his mind which many at first misunderstood has taken us places and into spaces and have surely made the world rumble. A beautiful mind, that was not wasted!

CHAPTER 3

The Power of Thoughts

Did you know that the average person has about 12,000 to 60,000 thoughts per day, of which 80% are negative and 95% are the same thoughts from the day before?

A *thought* is an idea or opinion produced by or occurring suddenly in the mind. A light bulb goes on, and things start to make sense—or they don't. Whether positive or negative, a thought can take you down the rabbit hole of *what-ifs* and *how-comes*. I have often had many ideas—brilliant or not—of possible inventions, designs, and more; however, the 80% crept in and made me feel my ideas were unworthy, mixed in with doubts that my peers placed on me, which I began to believe.

I remember my "designer season"—and I say that loosely. You see, I went to fashion school, where I obtained a degree, but the process of learning how to use a sewing machine was not something I had patience for. So, I came up with the BRILLIANT idea to hand-sew designs. For some odd reason, I thought that would be easier than using a sewing machine. In the end, I learned that what is easy is not always worth it, that the very thing we try to run from may actually help to make us better.

My first design was a scarf. It was "designed" to keep your neck warm but also to be worn as a skirt during the fall months. What I did not take into consideration is that your neck measurements are not the same as your hips. (Hey, I did say I had some *self-proclaimed* "brilliant" ideas!) I would tell my peers my idea and show them my product, and I would be met with a sarcastic, "Oh, that's cute. I will definitely buy one when I get paid." Or "Who is your target market?" Or, in other words, *"Who is going to buy that?"* Those comments marinated in my mind. They made me feel I wasn't good enough and made me doubt my process. Later in life, I found myself thinking, *what would have happened if I had blocked out the negativity and kept going?*

Sometimes, when God gives you an idea that He wants to come to fruition, you must keep it to yourself until He gives you confirmation to share, because many times, the same people you share your thoughts with are afraid of you operating in your full potential. These are not people you want in your circle, life, and future. I can now look back and see that I no longer speak to the people I once shared my ideas with. God has a way of removing individuals from your life who are not meant to move with you into your next chapter. Write your chapter with the ideas you have received, give power to your thoughts, and allow them to illuminate your path. If that thought does not work, remember you have 59,999 more you can draw from. I have also learned, through this transcendent journey, that thoughts are attached to timing. The timing of your thoughts aligns with encounters with specific people, places, or things that can help elevate them. As mentioned before Ecclesiastes 3 1-11 (NIV) talks all about the beauty and importance of time. Even though my thought of creating these "designer scarfs" may have occurred suddenly, it could very well be that the timing was not yet right, that the thought had to mature.

Think about when we were younger and looked up at our parents and they seemed like *giants* or what we considered *old*. As you grew and matured you could see that though they were tall you have now become their height or even surpassed them; and what we considered *old*, is now met with "I am NOT old in my 30's." It all took time and maturity for us to see things in a different way. Though that thought of the *interchangeable* "designer scarf" has soon been forgotten; the lesson(s) it has taught has stayed with me. The lesson of creation and how powerful the mind truly is. What you think you become; in a way, I believe God was giving me a glimpse of my future by showing me that life too is interchangeable. That it flows and changes with moments, seasons and even people; bringing about new possibilities and growth. A thought that once did not make sense, now has meaning; a powerful meaning!

A MOMENT OF REFLECTION

Take 10 minutes to write down as many thoughts and ideas that come to mind. Reflect on them and challenge yourself to bring them into fruition.

A MOMENT OF REFLECTION

Keep going, you can do it!

Part II

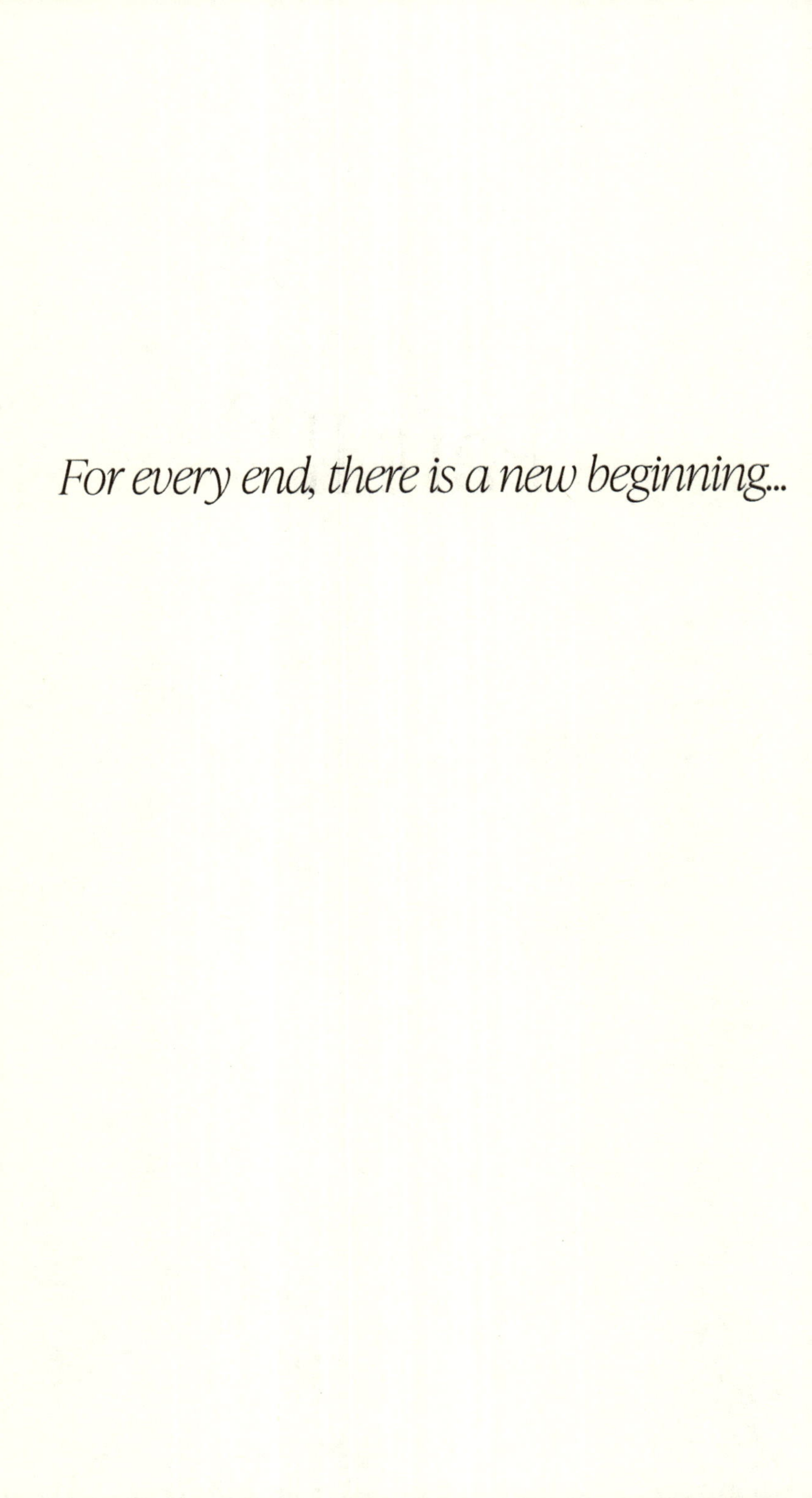
For every end, there is a new beginning...

The End of an Era

Look at a picture of yourself from 5, 10, or 15 years ago. What do you see? Most people would point out their physical features. They may have become healthier and stronger, their bodies may be more defined, their hair may be fuller, and their eyes brighter. Whatever the difference, we can all agree that there are changes, intentional or not, that have led to growth. Some people may think about the things they were once able to do that they wouldn't dare to do now, such as leave their house past 10 PM to go to a party, or pull an all-nighter without sleep and manage to make it to work on time in the morning, or eat $3 burritos at 4 AM. (Just writing this makes me want to say a prayer and take a nap.) This leads to the question: *When did you know you were changing?*

I can recall the moment I knew it was time to trade late nights and burritos for salads and face moisturizers. I was 23. The year was 2011. The hottest songs at the time were "Party

Rock Anthem" by LMFAO and "Firework" by Katy Perry, and if you had just gotten over a heartbreak, "Rolling in the Deep" by Adele was on repeat. My hair was in the "Snooki" puff, and I wore my favorite bandage dress from Forever 21 that hugged me in all the right and wrong places. Oh, and don't forget the platform pumps! Since social media wasn't as huge as it is now, I had every party promoter and DJ programmed into my phone. All it took was one simple text, "Where's the party at?" to send my phone down a text message frenzy. I *always* received messages from friends because I *always* knew where a party was happening. People knew where I would be, what time to contact me, and who I would be with. I guess, in a way, you can say I was predictable.

One Thursday evening in the summer, my best friend and I decided that we wanted to get our weekend started early. A long week of folding and putting away clothes for rude customers had awarded us a weekend to let loose. We decided to start by hanging out at our favorite bars and lounges on Clark and Division Street. If you are from Chicago or have ever visited, you know the famous street I am referring to. It is one long strip of bars and lounges, and no matter how you identify yourself, there is a place for you. It was notoriously known for being the street where everything stayed open until 4 AM.

That night, I hadn't gotten any text messages. The streets were unusually quiet for 10:30 p.m. When my friend and I walked into one of our favorite hangouts, it was dark and empty—but we were determined. "Rude Boy" by Rihanna was playing—we danced—but then an unexplained emptiness suddenly set in.

After 45 minutes, we decided to call it a night. We stopped at our favorite late-night restaurant, ordered two gyros and French fries, and sat on the stoop at the entrance. At that moment, we said almost simultaneously, "I don't want to do this anymore." What we thought we couldn't live without, and the people we thought would be in our lives forever, felt like the end of an era—dark, lonely, and empty. We realized we didn't just want to live—we wanted to create a legacy. For that to happen, we had to change.

That night changed the entire trajectory of my life. Today, not one person can predict what my weekends will look like. (I can't even predict what my weekdays will be like!) Today, I am no longer asked, "Where's the party at?"—and that feels good! Life should not feel predictable. Though having a routine is nice, and it can keep us on the straight and narrow, it may also keep us in a cycle. We can compare this to a washer and dryer whose function is to spin in a circle to make our clothes clean, but there are other functions on those machines that are able to do things outside the norm. Give yourself permission to explore the different functionalities within yourself. Discover the gifts you have within that make you special, then share those gifts to help others do the same; this creates change and change creates a cycle where action and adaptation are ongoing.

The end of an era is a new beginning. Whether met with fear or bravery, know that since you made the decision to move forward, God is showing that you are ready. Inhale, Exhale, Step Forward, and Welcome!

The Ripple Effect...

I found a pebble in the sand
I placed it in my hand
I felt as if I was holding on to my every dream and aspiration
What a sensation it was
I felt joy and happiness
I saw opportunities being endless
A deep feeling that is hard to explain
I heard a whisper in my ear
to trust and have no fear
because this dream would impact generations
but for this to happen
I need to be a captain and let go
of what I know
and trust that better will come
so
I released that pebble
and like a game
I moved to another level
and now generations can revel
in that pebble
that rippled back to me.

The Ripple Effect...

-Erika Degraffinreaidt

The Ripple Effect

There Is Life in the Rippling...

When you skip a pebble across a body of water, it will ripple. During a ripple, water molecules do not move away from the rock; they actually move up and down. When they move up, they drag the molecules next to them up; when they move down, they drag the molecules next to them down.

Every choice we make, good or bad, causes a ripple effect. Every decision we have ever made has, knowingly or unknowingly, caused a ripple effect that has affected us as individuals and/or those around us. Earlier, I mentioned that my grandmother, "Granny," the matriarch of my family, made the decision, in the late 1950's to move from Greenwood, Mississippi, during segregation and the racial uprising over the murder of Emmett Till. In the 1940s, many African Americans migrated to the Northeast, West, and Midwest searching for a better life. This was called the

Great Migration. My granny moved to the south suburbs of Chicago, Illinois, where she went on to birth five children, one being my wonderful mother. My grandmother's decision caused a ripple effect across generations, allowing her children to do great things and then their children to do even greater things.

Let's Dive Deeper...

For a positive ripple effect to occur, we must feel an inner and outer disturbance that causes us to decide to change who we are or our surroundings, which, in turn, disturbs the larger system. This gives reason to the saying, "Think long and hard before making a decision," because, as much as we would love to think choices only affect us, they don't. This can be applied to Rosa Parks, who refused to give up her seat on the segregated bus, and to Martin Luther King Jr., who had a dream, which became a dream of millions. Rosa Parks' and Dr. King's thoughts, visions, and actions rippled throughout generations and nations and embedded their names in history forever. Do you think they knew that the pebble they had thrown into the river would cause this many ripples? I'm sure they are looking down from the heavens in awe of not just how things turned out, but also how they encouraged others to throw their own pebble(s) into a large system to create change as well.

Throughout my life, tossing pebbles into the sea, with hopes that ripples would come back to me, resulted in those ripples returning tenfold. One decision I made 13 years ago has rippled back over and over again: moving from my hometown of Bartlett, Illinois, to New York and now Los Angeles. I am still in awe of the doors that swung open and stayed open from that decision. It affected those around me, including my parents: they found themselves having "parental anxiety," worrying about my well-being. I do believe I may have been the cause of a few gray hairs on their heads. Though that could be seen as a small negative, my decision opened doors for other people, as well as myself. It opened up a role at the company that I left for another person to make their mark. It opened up a home for someone to live in. It propelled me forward and has allowed me to impact the larger system with my work, thoughts, and dreams. It is time to release your pebble because, if held on to, it will affect the system at large. Release it and watch it ripple back in a way you could never imagine.

CHAPTER 6

Follow the Leader

As children, we played many games: tag, duck, duck, goose, and my favorite, follow the leader. One thing these games have in common is that someone is chosen to lead. At six years old, being chosen was a heavy pressure and responsibility. I can still remember the butterflies in my stomach and clasping my little hands tightly, thinking, "Please choose me!" I remember thinking of strategies I would use if I were the leader. In duck, duck, goose, I would take my time going around the circle of children, allowing them to wait in anticipation, making sure to touch their heads gently. I say this because there was always one child who was a little heavy-handed, who would slap my head every time he went around the circle (hand-to-barrette contact against a freshly tied pigtail was *not* a good feeling). Being considerate was a strategy of mine, as well as ensuring I wasn't just choosing someone because they were a friend, but because I felt they were qualified. These types of attributes have always been important to me and have carried through to adulthood. I guess you could say that I really took the game to heart.

In follow the leader (for those who aren't familiar with the rules of this game), one child is chosen to lead. The rest of the children line up behind the leader and must copy all of the leader's actions. This game translated heavily into how I've always chosen my friends, especially in high school, where seemingly everyone thinks they are a leader. As teen-agers, we tend to follow those who outwardly portray what we want to be known for; for example, the quarterback on a high school football team. The quarterback is the leader on and off the field, and those on the team follow their lead. (This also goes for women and persons whose gender iden-tity is not fixed.) They must look like them, act like them, and move like them because they are seen as a reflection of them. I would always watch my brothers, who were football players and team leaders. I would see how everyone followed them. I could not wait until I was seen and chosen to lead. At that time, I wasn't fully awakened to my leadership qual-ities, and I would gravitate toward those seen as "outsiders"; however, inwardly, they were just like me: a leader patiently waiting in anticipation to be chosen.

Some of the greatest leaders of our time had to go through a season of not being seen, of being overlooked, in order to build the courage to rise up. Even though it took some time, when I moved into adulthood and started working in corporate environments, I made a point during job interviews to ask the manager, "What are the greatest attributes every manager should have to effectively lead a team?" (This is a daunting question for those deemed a leader by default and given the title of manager.) If a manager answered the question in depth, I instantly knew they not only had a passion for what they did, but they would also be more willing to show me how to be a better leader. That is important, especially in today's world, where following individuals, specifically on social media, will make someone think they are a leader because the larger the number, the more "influence" the world believes they have. In reality, quality will always mean more than quantity. An individual may have thousands of followers, but where are they being led? One should always follow someone who will lead them to be better and who will enrich their lives in a way that will ripple through time. That is the point of life: to become a better version of yourself with each day you are given.

I challenge you to evaluate the people you are following in your daily life and through social media. Ask yourself, *"Are these people leading me to be greater? Am I learning to enhance my leadership qualities through them? Or are they leading me nowhere?"* If you are unable to find a great leader to follow, become the leader you wish to see. That's what I call a great game of following the leader!

Part III

A MOMENT OF REFLECTION

Reflect on a time when you were recognized for being a leader. How has that helped others rise up to do the same?

A MOMENT OF REFLECTION

The bench is warm, but my name has been called...

CHAPTER 7

Benchwarmers

On every sports team, there are players drafted to play and win, and then there are those who serve as substitutes, representations of the team, but in many cases, they never get to play—they are the benchwarmers.

On your individual journey, you will encounter people who seem to be on your team, who will root for you when you are winning, but inwardly, they wish they were playing the game. Do not get me wrong; there are many people who genuinely want to see you win, but from my experience on this creative journey, I have found that many find it hard to continue to root for you when you are in a season of non-stop winning. They may have been very vocal in the beginning, showing their support by liking your posts, sharing your story on social media, and coming to your events, only to, over time, quietly fade into the shadows and sit on the bench and just watch. As a player who is doing the work to leverage the team, it makes you wonder why they have suddenly stopped. I will say that when you see people rooting for you and then suddenly stop without reason, it affects you, no matter how strong you are. I can only speak for myself, but oftentimes when this has happened, it made me feel like I was doing something wrong that resulted in their lack of support. The truth is, this is not your fault. You are doing nothing wrong. Do not feel bad. Do not allow them to keep you from your purpose. Keep winning for your team (your family and friends)—for those who really want to see you win.

The true reason people become benchwarmers is that something inside them is not able to accept seeing those they were once on the same level with, financially, educationally, or career-wise, surpass them. It makes them feel they are at a standstill or that their work isn't good enough. Their mindset should not block you from defending your position. You were chosen, and you accepted the position because you believed that your vision and tenacity would help bring the team to victory. I believe that people are put in the position to play because they have been prepared in previous seasons. YOU were prepared mentally, physically, and emotionally, which made you ready for the mission. Could you imagine if you had the success you have now five years ago? Ten years ago? I can't! I wouldn't know what to do with it. I wouldn't have been mature enough to make logical decisions, and I most certainly would not have known how to be a leader. I thank God that He sat me on that bench to watch and root for others until my name was called. As a benchwarmer, if you stay focused on what is happening in the game, and you continue to root for your teammates while still preparing on your own, your name will eventually be called. Once it has been called, you will now represent the team. That is the beauty of the calling and why every season, whether good or bad, is needed. It lays the groundwork for you to play in the game of life.

Your name has been called, so what's Next…

You respond by saying "Yes!' The next step is embracing a new identity. An important step that is often overlooked. As mentioned, you were once known as a *benchwarmer* without a name being attached. Once you accept the calling, God gives you a new name. God changed the name of several people in the bible, including Abram to Abraham, Sarai to Sarah, Simon to Peter. This signifies your spiritual transformation from darkness to light, your new destiny and that God has a specific plan for your life. God changes your name so you are not associated with the old version of yourself. Think about nicknames you were given when you were younger, they no longer fit the person that you are; but still family and friends will call you that name because that is who they know you as. When introducing yourself to friends in your adult years, most would not introduce nicknames especially if it was not endearing. I remember during my time of darkness, individuals would call me "E" or "E-Money" or "Sally Sue" all nicknames they decided to give me without my permission, which I never corrected and still responded to. It was only when I said yes to the calling that those individuals were no longer around and identifying with those names had no purpose. The calling comes with new meaning and growth.

Thirdly, which may be the hardest step is; *listening and obeying*. Just like a coach leading the team to victory, they give specific assignments and instructions in order to provide strategic direction to achieve victory against opponents. The coach is put in place for a reason, they have a broader view and can see what we have yet to experience. God is the coach of our life, he provides strategic advice and communicates with us daily through his word (bible), songs and even through people to help us stay in the game. All he asks in return is for obedience. The word obedience may seem *harsh* with limitations; but in actuality it comes with freedom and growth. As Matthew 7:13-14 (NIV) states "Enter through the narrow gate. For wide is the gate and broad is the road that leads to destruction, and many enter through it. But small is the gate and narrow the road that leads to life, and only a few find it." You are part of the few that said *yes* to the calling and went through the narrow gate and now are being led to a life of freedom.

Lastly, you allow your gifts to be of service to others, to lead them to victory. God called your name at this specific time, because he knew that people needed what was placed in you. As mentioned, I started in the entertainment industry as a fashion stylist. God gave me that gift and used me in that area for 8 years. (spiritual meaning of 8 is resurrection and a new spiritual reality) Allowing me to be a light in an industry that is widely known for its darkness. Having the opportunity to work internationally being of service to hundreds of people, to tell hundreds of visual stories while sharing the goodness of God. Though God has shifted me into new areas within the industry, the pebble that I threw into the water, caused a ripple, which I am still feeling the effects of. It is your gift that keeps on giving long after it's done that makes all of this worth it. Teamwork makes the dream work!

CHAPTER 8

Hometown Glory

Singing B-A-R-T-L-E-T-T
What's that spell?
BARTLETT!
Go HAWKS!

This cheer has been embedded in my soul since I first heard it as an adolescent during our hometown sports games—words that not only expressed pride in my hometown but also the traditions and people that made that town *home*.

When I think of home, I think of peace, freedom, love, joy, and Mama's cooking. It is a place we return to when feeling weary; it is a place of familiarity. But what if we were to look inward for a sense of home? In a world that pressures us through music and social media, which are constantly telling us to escape our reality, wouldn't it be great to just turn inward when outside distractions become too much to bear? What if I told you it is much easier than you think and that it doesn't have any bad side effects?

There is a secret to finding your inner home… The process is similar to finding a physical home. We have all gone through the tedious process of house hunting. The main questions we ask ourselves are as follows:

- *Is the location good?*
- *Do I feel safe?*
- *Is it within my budget?*
- *Is this a place where I can see myself living long-term?*

These questions often reveal our non-negotiables, so let's apply these same questions to our internal homes.

As I have gotten older, I have learned to truly listen to my intuition in order to keep my home safe. Our intuition gives us a physical sensation, such as a stomachache, or it makes us anxious, indicating that the decision we are about to make may or may not be in our best interest. I can think of a number of times, especially in my younger years, that I ignored my intuition and ended up in a sticky situation that only the grace of God got me out of. Can you recall a time you ignored your intuition? I think we all can: listening and following those feelings has saved us from a repeat cycle. Therefore, it is important to keep your internal location clear of things that could harm it, numb it, or give a distorted feeling that keeps you from being aware of where you are.

Next, when looking for our home, safety is a priority. We tend to gravitate towards environments that foster security for ourselves and family. Have you ever been in a place where you constantly feel the need to look over your shoulder? It is uncomfortable, uneasy, and stressful. A safe environment gives you a peace of mind that extends to all aspects of your life. It is not just about physical safety, but it is also about the emotional well-being that comes with being secure in your surroundings. Safety is being in the arms of Jesus, as like a child in its mother's womb, it is protected; it is home.

Thirdly, we ensure that we have a budget to keep us aligned and not overspend. There is nothing worse than creating a budget and not staying within it. When we over-spend, we reap the negative consequences: we feel stretched, stressed, and worried. Relating this to our internal homes, if we overwork ourselves and stretch past our limitations, we place ourselves in the negative. When we are in the negative, what use are we? How can we pour from an empty cup? In a world where everything is done in excess, we are told to have more, work more, and spend more, even if it is at the cost of our well-being. While having more may *look* greater, what *hol* has it deepened within? So, stay within your internal budget, know what your worth is, and do not spend it on people, plac-es, or things that are not worthy of it. As the good old saying goes: *If it costs your joy, peace, and happiness, it is too expensive.*

We only have ONE internal home, so we must be in-tentional with what we place in it. We must furnish it with nice things that make us feel good and that represent who we are, and take our time and purchase things that make it feel complete. We must not just put any and everything in our home. Whatever you put into your mind, body, soul, and home, you become, so let's feed ourselves love and affirmations that allow us to become our Highest Self. Finding and establishing a home that has peace, freedom, love, joy, and Mama's cooking means finding God, and once you allow God to move into your home, you are complete! Once you are complete, it is hard to go back or fill your home with things that once made it feel "empty." As James 1:4 (NIV) states, "Let perseverance finish its work so you may be mature and complete, not lacking anything." Let your words sing the melody of your heart's desire, bringing you to a place of wholeness.

CHAPTER 9

On Your Mark

"On your mark, get set…GO!" Those words rang in my ears throughout my entire high school track career. I still hear them to this day…I feel my heart beating fast from nervousness and excitement, and there is the doubt that crosses my mind, making me question my preparedness as I silently tell myself to stay focused and not worry about the competition standing to the left and right of me.

It's crazy how it's been over fifteen years, and those same feelings and lessons I felt on that mark can still be applied to my present life. How many of you can honestly say you have felt doubt and nervousness about the track you are on, and worried about the people around you? It's a normal thing, especially in today's society, with social media saying you are not enough if you do not have certain things—even making us envious of our friends because we see them living a life we wish we had. I'm here to say that, when we see our friends winning or celebrities living this AMAZING life, we have to remember they only tend to show the good aspects. We start to compete with those around us, trying to outwork them, outdo them, and outspend them, all for show, not truly knowing the internal battles they are fighting or the sacrifices they have made to have that lifestyle. Many of those sacrifices may have come with turmoil or regret being done in the dark and not yet being brought to light. As the book of Luke 8:17 (NIV) states "For there is nothing hidden that will not be disclosed, and nothing concealed that will not be known or brought out into the open."

In a race, when the runners are on their mark, no athlete truly knows the training their competitors endured to get there. I, for one, can admit that there were many times I stepped on that mark, fresh off an injury, or not feeling my best, but I felt the need to appear as if I was doing fine, even to the point of overdoing my warm-up exercises, because I wanted to show my competition I was someone they didn't want to mess with. In reality, my injuries were not quite healed. What I tried to hide came to light, when the same competition I was trying to impress in a previous season saw that I wasn't participating in the current season (due to my injury being exposed). It revealed the truth behind what was hidden. Sometimes God will bring things to light to bring about humility which then opens the way for grace and exaltation and a testimony. If I did not go through the hidden seasons I would not have this testimony; I would not have the wisdom, or words to inspire, the stories that were told to make this book; Transcend. It is through the darkness that you find your light.

Never believe everything you see because filters, smiles, and perfected images can often be falsified perceptions. It is so important that you stay in your lane and stay focused on what's ahead of you. When you hear, "On your mark," it's just you in your assigned lane; do what you have been prepared to do. It doesn't matter if you are the first person off the line or a little delayed; what matters is that you start and finish, and that you do it at your own pace.

Finishing the Race

Many moons ago, when I ran track & field, I remember my coach saying, "You have to finish the race. No matter how tired or behind you are, you have to finish." Imagine hearing that, especially on the last stretch of a 4x400 relay when your entire body is telling you to give up, but your mind is saying that you have to keep going because it's not just about you but also about finishing for your team.

Those words have followed me throughout my personal and professional life. They have given me the strength to keep pushing when things get hard. They have allowed me to live a selfless life. As much as we would love to think that our actions only affect us, we are most certainly wrong. Things we set our mind to do, whether on a small or large scale, will consequently affect those around us. Throughout this journey, specifically working in the entertainment industry, I have seen that one idea created by a writer, a story written, has produced work for dozens of people. From taking an idea from their mind, that at first may have been misunderstood, through trial and error, doubt, life experiences, brought about a team of directors, crew and actors to bring those words to life for us to see. By seeing things from others brought into fruition, it gives us the hope and faith to keep moving forward. No matter how impossible it seems. The word *impossible* actually means *i'm-possible.* A saying coined by British actress Audrey Hepburn.

Take this moment to speak life into yourself and your dreams. Say " I am Infinite, I have Purpose, Anything and Everything that I do, carries endless Possibilities."

I encourage you to finish the race, no matter how far behind or ahead you are. Finish for your team, finish for your fans, and finish for the person you currently are and who you are yet to become. This race of life is a marathon, so don't worry about the distance, the time, or competing. Run at your own pace.

In full transparency, the book that you now hold in your hands has been a *long* race, 3.5 years to be exact. It started as an idea, during a 3 month period of isolation, while doing theatre in Lanesboro, Minnesota. A town whose population as of the 2022 census was estimated at 829 people. As you can imagine it was quite a shock for me being a "city girl" especially because my high school graduation class was at least 1,000 people and I've always lived in environments whose population were in the millions.

Sitting in a room with myself, my thoughts and a pen and paper seemed like my only options. (Even though the town is famously known for its outdoor recreation and its theatre scene). When I was not in rehearsal or performing I stayed to myself. I know many may question "where my castmates were?" Well to answer your question, they were *around*, with their *friends*, those they had cultivated relationships with months prior to me arriving. I was the "newcomer" to the group, which if you have ever been in this situation it feels like a game of "Survivor." I felt that every question that was asked, every task that was given was for me to prove that I belonged. As I was not just the "city girl" I was different in many ways the town was not quite used to. The questions and tasks that were asked, I now know were due to a lack of knowledge from things that they had never been exposed to. Naturally, questions and curiosity would come from what is unknown.

Though I thought I was in Lanesboro, Minnesota for theatre, God used those months that were unknown to me at the time to sow a seed; that took years to harvest; that I am now reaping the rewards from. God uses isolation to cleanse you from distractions and prepare you for a greater purpose. God isolated Elijah by allowing him to flee into the wilderness to prepare him for intense future missions. Daniel was thrown in the lion's den surrounded by lions (though for one night) he endured the loneliness and a night of waiting, through terrifying isolation where his life was at stake only for God to show him that he was protected. Jesus went to the wilderness for 40 days after his baptism; where he endured intense solitude, spiritual testing by Satan all in preparation for his public ministry. These are a few examples (though there are many others in the Bible) that show how God isolates his best.

The actions of those I was surrounded with opened my mind to seek, explore and question who I am and the world I live in which led to me finding my *super power*. The Super Power being my experiences, leading to you finding yours, in hope of your Transcendence.

It's important to finish strong. The race is long, and sometimes you are tired, but BELIEVE, BELIEVE, BELIEVE that everything you have gone through has fully prepared you for your destiny. God did not bring you this far to leave you. Finish the race!

A MOMENT OF REFLECTION

Your name has been called, now reflect on all that you have learned to stay in the race.

A MOMENT OF REFLECTION

Just like any race,
once it has ended,
you start training for the next one.

Transcend, the memoir, is only the start to this race…

Stay tuned.

APPENDIX

Chapter 1: The Waiting Room
The Message: Allow yourself time and space to be transformed. Each stage of transcending will be different; some days will be hard, some easy, and some manageable, but what comes from your waiting is beautiful—transformative: it can shape new realities that you need not distort or escape from. Waiting isn't punishment; it's preparation.

Chapter 2: A Beautiful Mind
The Message: Do not allow doubts about your different way of thinking to hinder your greatness. Every experience you have affects your thought processes. Each thought inspires an action to change not only ourselves but also those around us to create a better world.

Chapter 3: The Power of Thoughts
The Message: Stay the course. Hold on to the vision, even if others cannot see it. Start your mornings with gratitude. If a negative thought tries to creep in, tell yourself, "I am

Worthy, I am Loved, My thoughts have Value, and I have a Purpose. I Belong Here, and I am Here to Stay."

Chapter 4: The End of an Era

<u>The Message</u>: To create your legacy, you must be willing to let go of who you are and the life you planned to have the life that is waiting for you. Trust your intuition. Know when it is time to evolve. When you recognize this and work toward change, you are letting God know you are ready to shift. You will be working together to create the life He has destined for you. Your evolution helps others to grow and mature. Wake up from living a "safe" and predictable life and say, "I am ready for change!"

Chapter 5: The Ripple Effect

<u>The Message</u>: Be willing to throw your pebble into the water. Trust that it will ripple back to you bigger and better. Take a moment to think about a time in your life when you made a decision that affected your entire life and that of others. How has that decision made you better? Ponder on that thought and journal about it. You will see that growth came from tossing that pebble. Whether it was mentally, physically, emotionally, or financially, it created change, and with change came growth.

Chapter 6: Follow the Leader

<u>The Message</u>: Be a reflection of the leader you would like to become. Ask questions. Become comfortable with being

uncomfortable. Pay attention to those you spend time with and who you follow in your daily life, including on social media. You will begin to mimic their actions, words, and thoughts, so make sure the people you are following are a direct reflection of who you would like to become.

Chapter 7: Benchwarmers

<u>The Message</u>: Do not fall when the pressure of winning and others' lack of support get to you. Know that your winning is because of the preparation you did in previous seasons. The time you spent on the bench waiting for your name to be called, while still rooting for your teammates, is why you are in your position right now. You didn't allow time or hard work to tarnish your heart. You made it through the training—this is why you are winning! KEEP IT UP. Continue working toward your dreams, trusting the process, and enjoying the journey until your name is called to lead your team to victory.

Chapter 8: Hometown Glory

<u>The Message</u>: Fill your home with things that make you feel good. Look in the mirror and say to yourself, "I love you. I embrace my flaws because I am human. I am fully dedicating myself to healing and wholeness, meaning I will evolve. As long as God is in my home, I will never fail. Fill me up, God; I invite you to live in my dwelling place."

Chapter 9: On Your Mark

<u>The Message</u>: Do not see those around you as competition. Stay focused on the lane God assigned to you and designed *for* you because He knows when you will finish your race. God paces us to protect us and to prepare us for what we were placed on this earth to do; He said, "Before I formed you in the womb I knew you, before you were born I set you apart; I appointed you as a prophet to the nations" (Jeremiah 1:5 [NIV]).

ABOUT THE AUTHOR

Erika Degraffinreaidt is an multi-disciplinary international artist from Bartlett, Illinois whose work spans over 15 years within the entertainment industry, from being an international fashion stylist and photographer to an actress who is a current member of SAG-AFTRA and the Television Academy. Erika uses her social media platforms to share her journey and motivate individuals across the world to live a free and inspirational life. *Transcend* is the product of every stone thrown at Erika—every trial on her journey—that she has used to build for good.

Erika resides in Los Angeles, California, where she enjoys philanthropy with her church, as well as traveling, writing, photography, acting, and transcending. She holds on to the Word of God and thanks God for not giving up on His promises.

FrenchVendette